BEYOND
BETRAYAL

STANDING IN THE MIDST OF ADVERSITY

ADDIE J. McCAFFERTY

Beyond Betrayal
Standing in the Midst of Adversity

By
Addie J. McCafferty

Pure Thoughts Publishing, LLC

In Memory of My Mother

I write this book in memory of my mother, Gertrude Brown who taught me how to be resilient in the things of life. Though our early years were rocky to say the least, she proved to be one of my biggest fans. She always encouraged me in my endeavors. She also made sure she let me know her thoughts about something be it good or bad. I will forever miss her presence in my life. She was indeed a voice of reason and definitely one of my ravens.

Missing you Momma

December 1929 - March 2013

Cover design by KLF Design Firm
Editor: Integrity2 Editing Services
All Scripture quotations are taken from the
Holy Bible, King James Version (KJV),
unless otherwise noted.
Collins English Dictionary - Complete &
Unabridged 2012 Digital Edition
© William Collins Sons & Co. Ltd. 1979,
1986 © HarperCollins
Publishers 1998, 2000, 2003, 2005, 2006,
2007, 2009, 2012

This document is geared towards providing
exact and reliable information in regards
to the topic and issue covered. The
publication is sold with the idea that the
publisher is not required to render
accounting, officially permitted, or
otherwise, qualified services. If advice is
necessary, legal or professional, a
practiced individual in the profession
should be ordered.
From a Declaration of Principles which was

accepted and approved equally by a Committee of the American Bar Association and a Committee of Publishers and Associations.

In no way is it legal to reproduce, duplicate, or transmit any part of this document in either electronic means or in printed format. Recording of this publication is strictly prohibited and any storage of this document is not allowed unless with written permission from the publisher. All rights reserved.

The information provided herein is stated to be truthful and consistent, in that any liability, in terms of inattention or otherwise, by any usage or abuse of any policies, processes, or directions contained within is the solitary and utter responsibility of the recipient reader. Under no circumstances will any legal responsibility or blame be held against the publisher for any reparation, damages, or monetary loss due to the information herein, either directly or indirectly. Respective authors own all copyrights not held by the publisher.

The information herein is offered for informational purposes solely, and is universal as so. The presentation of the information is without contract or any type of guarantee assurance.

The trademarks that are used are without any consent, and the publication of the trademark is without permission or backing by the trademark owner. All trademarks and brands within this book are for clarifying purposes only and are the owned by the owners themselves, not affiliated with this document.

All Scripture quotation, unless otherwise indicated, are taken from the Holy Bible, New International VersionÒ. NIVÒ. Copyright Ó 1973, 1978, 1984 by International Bible Society. Used by permission of Zondervan Publishing House.

ISBN: 978-1-943409-04-4

Dedication

I dedicate this book to those who prayed for me, loved me, encouraged me, and helped me to laugh in the midst of my adversity. To those of you who have and are facing betrayal of any kind, know that God is faithful and that He will not allow you to suffer any more than you can bear. God is true to His promises. Everything that you have endured is working for your good and His glory. Believe me; I know you may not see it right now; however God has a plan in the midst of your pain. , STAND in the midst of your adversity and get Beyond Betrayal. *Blessings!!!!*

Acknowledgements

To my Heavenly Father (my Daddy) thank you for loving and protecting me. To my cousin Adrienne, your prayers and encouragement are worth far more to me than rubies. Without your intercession on behalf of the family where would we be – Thank you. To Trudy, my super talented baby sister – you have been my biggest fan – Thank you for your consistent and unconditional love, I so appreciate you. To Jennifer - thank you for being a strength to me in times of weakness throughout my trials with our mother. I probably would not be here if it wasn't for you. To Esther and Ian, you have truly been like a sister and a brother to me throughout our twenty-six years of friendship – Thank you for your love, support and sharing your family with me and giving me a home away from home. To Kim Blackmon, Katrina Spigner, Kim Brooks and Dr. Nicholas Cooper-Lewter – thank you for your love, encouragement and the dynamics that each of you add individually and collectively to my life. I thank God for the gifts that each of you bring to the table. To Pastor Greg and Jan Railey – thank you for your love, prayers, support, leadership and friendship. This type of love coming from leadership means more to me than you guys could ever know. Finally, "now thanks

be unto God, who always causeth us to triumph in
Christ…" (2 Corn. 2:14).

Betrayal: v.

1. to disappoint the hopes or expectations of; be disloyal to:

2. to be unfaithful in guarding, maintaining, or fulfilling:

late 13c., bitrayen "mislead, deceive, betray," from be- + obsolete Middle English tray, from Old French traine "betrayal, deception, deceit," from trair (Modern French trahir) "betray, deceive," from Latin tradere "hand over," from trans- "across" (see trans-) + dare "to give" (see date (n.1)).

Dictionary.com

Table of Contents

Dedication vii

Acknowledgements viii

Foreword..13

Endorsements..14

Introduction 16

The Journey Begins 19

I Thought They Loved Me...24

The Betrayal of Marriage 28

Family Betrayal 32

So Called Friends...36

Preparation for the Test 40

When Leadership Betrays You....................................45

The Betrayal Continues 51

Beyond Betrayal   Addie J. McCafferty

Overcoming the Betrayal..58

Conclusion..60

Scriptures for Healing and Encouragement...............61

About the Author...63

Foreword

It is with great joy that I am afforded this privilege of recommending to you not just a book, not just a story...but the life, mantle and anointed deposit of God revealed in this author, woman of God, prophetess and friend, Addie J. McCafferty! As a spiritual father in her life over the past 14+years, I have had the privilege to watch the story that is unfolded on these pages become a living reality in her life, struggles, victories; but most importantly, in her infectious smile and laugh, as well as the way she loves people...all people!

A wise and seasoned mentor in my life once said, every David will have at least one Saul in their lives, and every Joseph will walk through the betrayal of those they have loved dearest and deepest! But the process is more important than the details...for it produces in you an eternal weight of glory. This is that kind of story! In walking through these pages, it will introduce you to that kind of glory! Enjoy and be changed and blessed by Addie's heart-rending life's experiences!

Apostle Greg Railey

Endorsements

Greetings,

I know Addie Lewis - McCafferty as a Godly woman who wants to help others overcome the odds and Be and Become all God created them to be. Her story is about the Providence of God. God reserves the right to transform the worse experiences into something good. Be inspired as you too stand with this lady of God.

Rev. Dr. Nicholas Cooper-Lewter aka The Soul Whisperer

Wow!!!

Watch the power of God powerfully manifest when bitterness, hurt, and resentment are expected. The fruit of peace, forgiveness, trust and intimacy with the lord are displayed as you read through the pages of this book. A. Jacque demonstrates through powerful testimony that it is only by His love and pursuit of her that betrayal doesn't take root and that love flourishes.

Jennifer M. Olson

*"The saddest thing about betrayal is
that it never comes from your enemies"*
Unknown

Introduction

Everyone has experienced betrayal at one point in their lifetime. If you have not, consider yourself blessed. The most hurtful thing is that betrayal seldom comes from your enemies. Betrayal, often, comes from those we love and trust. The worst betrayal is usually in the form of our friends, family members such as a mother, father, sister, brother, and spouse. Betrayal can also come from those we entrust our spiritual accountability to like a pastor, their spouse, the elders of the church and other Christians etc. No matter the source betrayal can be devastating.

This book is a powerful representation of the Father bringing victory, healing and deliverance beyond betrayal. It depicts how a personal relationship with God, a determination to move beyond the pain and making a choice to forgive are the key elements to walking through adverse circumstances that the enemy meant for your destruction. What is significant is that even in the midst of the trial God is right there waiting for you to grab hold of His hand. There is a song that says, precious Lord take my hand, lead me on and let me stand. God is there to guide you to that place of healing and wholeness.

I'm here to let you know that there is hope in the midst of the pain. God deserves the right to turn evil into good. Know for certain that God sees you and love's you. I know it doesn't always feel good, however believe me God is working for your good.

I never get too worried because I know that God works in everything for my good. Two mantras that I often quote are (1) "love like you've never been hurt" and (2) "when life serves you lemons make lemonade." When you apply these two mantras to your life, in the midst of adversity they will lift your spirit and remind you that God work together for your good and squeeze a final blessing out of anything. Some people often say "that which doesn't make you bitter will make you better." Most of all, I am encouraging you to stand in the midst of your adversity and get beyond the betrayal.

When you allow yourself to soar your perspective on things change. If things are looking discouraging you are not soaring high enough. #flyhigh

#likeaneagle #AJM

The Journey Begins

This is where the journey began. I was born and raised in the ghetto on the South Side of Chicago, Illinois. The funny thing was we were poor, however I did not realize it. My oldest sister Jennifer and mother were resilient and creative in the midst of our being poor. I had eight other siblings. Unfortunately, three of my siblings are now deceased (one sister and two brothers).

There was a big age gap between the first six and the last three of the sisters and brothers. I am next to the youngest. My mother's mother died when my mother was six years old and my mother spent her youth in foster homes. When my mother began to have children she really did not know how to be a "mom."

We did not grow up going to church, nor did we have any concept about religion. We were street wise, doing whatever we thought we were big and bad enough to do. After living with my grandmother on my father's side until it was time for me to attend school, the majority of my youth was spent with my oldest sister who raised me. I went back and forth from living with her to living with my mother. My mother was abusive verbally, emotionally, and sometimes physically.

This was the first betrayal. The main person that was supposed to love and protect me did just the opposite and betrayed the love of a child for a parent. No matter what I did, it was not good enough. I was called "b#%$@" and told that I would never be "s!#@".

This type of aggression towards me, because of the spirit of God within me, seemed to fuel me to want to do even better, to excel to the top of my game. It was this type of aggression that pushed me to be the best that I could be. I was determined to prove her wrong and it worked. I graduated with honors throughout all my primary school years and even through college.

I fought hard not to allow the abuse to make my heart bitter. Once I became aware of God moving in my life and being "born again" as a Christian, I went home to Chicago to confront my mother concerning the way I was treated and to forgive her. I wasn't looking for her to apologize (even though that would have been nice). I forgave my mother so that I could walk into the blessings that I knew God had for my life.

My father and mother were divorced. He was a functional alcoholic which ultimately led to his untimely death. I was in my late twenties at the time. I would go by his apartment to check on him, making sure he had food and was being taken care of. In spite of his alcoholism I loved my dad and I believed he loved me.

Reflections

Has anyone such as a parent or guardian ever betrayed you?

_____

_____

_____

_____

_____

_____

What was your response to being betrayed?

_____

_____

_____

_____

_____

_____

_____

What would it be like to be healed from the effects of the betrayal?

_____

_____

_____

_____

_____

_____

If you don't transform your pain you will transmit it...unknown #IJS

I Thought They Loved Me

I married at the age of seventeen; right after high school to a man that was six years older than me. I graduated in June of 1980, had a big wedding in August, turned eighteen in November and my husband got killed in March of 1981 just eight months after we got married. I grew up so fast!! The sad thing was in this marriage I was betrayed once again. I was so naive. My husband had a temper problem, an appetite for women and was quick to start a fight. I had gotten so fed up (not to mention I had a bad temper too) that a week before he had got killed, I tried to kill him. Just think I would have been in jail for something that was his ultimate end.

During the time of my marriage to my husband I thought his family loved me. They were always so kind and appeared to be concerned about me. During the planning stage of the wedding they were very helpful and did whatever they could to make sure the wedding was successful. They even hosted a bridal shower in my honor.

As I think back I realize just how oblivious I was to the real meaning of love. I was naive and trusted people to do what they said. I really thought that they loved me. However, upon my husband's death I saw a side of them that I did not know existed.

The beneficiary of his insurance policy was his mother. Once this was discovered the love that they were showing to me changed. This was betrayal knocking at my door once again.

Reflections

Have you ever thought that someone loved you and realized that they didn't?

_____

_____

_____

_____

_____

_____

How did that make you feel?

_____

_____

_____

_____

_____

What would healing from that experience look like?

_____

_____

_____

_____

_____

_____

What's amazing is when you think you are at the end; you discover there's another provision in place..AJM
#mygodisawesome

The Betrayal of Marriage

I was eighteen years old and living on my own. I began to hear about how God could make me whole and successful. People had told me you needed to be in church to have a connection with God, but I soon realized that I had always had a connection with God. I however was not ready for a full commitment to God. I really did not know what a full commitment required. I just was not ready.

Five years later I married again to a high school boyfriend who had recently joined the military. When I left Chicago I had a plan. I never experienced the unconditional love from my mother. I was looking for a means of escape. Getting married seemed to be the perfect way to escape to me. I thought I would marry this man, go to Texas and then find the soul mate of my life in which I would be with forever. Well, it worked out just that way but not the way I thought it would be. I met Jesus within three months of getting to Texas. Jesus has not left me, nor have I left Him since!

My husband at the time knew of my true feelings towards him before we got married. He knew that I was not in love with him, but once I became "born again" as some call it, I asked God to give me a love for him that a wife was supposed to have for her husband. This was necessary seeing that my plan A went out the window. The God ordained love lasted for the next twenty years.

We were in Texas for only one year due to the loss of our first pregnancy. The four month pregnancy resulted in emergency surgery which almost took my life. The military moved us to Germany to get us into a different environment. We stayed in Germany for the next six years and there my love and knowledge of the Lord grew stronger and stronger and so did my trials. These years are what I call my growing years.

Through my relationship with God I grew to understand who I was and who I was created to be. I learned the importance of integrity and character. I allowed the word of God to change me from the inside out. All of these things came about from the trials that I encountered.

My husband began to do things he had never done before that tested the new me. His activity in his fraternal affiliation and infidelity had him doing things he had never done before. Some tests I passed and some I didn't. We ended up separating while overseas. These actions of my husband put a desire in me to leave Germany to give me the space I needed to heal. I allowed God to deal with the issues and attitudes within me that would hinder me from becoming the woman of God that I am today.

Reflections

Have you ever been betrayed by a spouse or a
significant other?

_____

_____

_____

_____

_____

_____

How did you process it or did you?

_____

_____

_____

_____

_____

_____

Is this still an area in which you need healing?

_____

_____

_____

_____

_____

_____

Even when we don't understand all God want us to do is Trust Him!!
<u>*#quittryingtofigureitout*</u> *#AJM*

Family Betrayal

When I had given my life to The Lord I was so excited I called one of my siblings. As a result of my commitment to God I was told in so many words they would cut me off. They also told me to remember how they cut off another family member when they committed their life to God. I was devastated.

Then the Scripture came to me in Mark 10:29-30 "and Jesus answered and said, verily I say unto you, there is no man that hath left house, or brethren, or sisters, or father, or mother, or wife, or children, or lands, for my sake, and the gospel's but he shall receive an hundredfold now in this time......" God will give you a family that has nothing to do with your natural bloodline. He will connect you with your spiritual DNA. These relationships can be even stronger than any natural bloodline connections.

Once I returned from Germany my family saw the change in my life and how I developed into this compassionate loving person. Until Christ touched my life it was my understanding that in order to survive I believed I had to be hard and cold. This change had a domino effect in the lives of my siblings.

Today all my siblings are serving the Lord. This is a miracle seeing where we all have come from. A relationship with a loving God is the key. This is not to say that I do not experience trials and tribulations, I just know who the who is inside of me. This mindset allows me to move beyond the betrayal and continue to stand.

Reflections

Have your siblings betrayed you?

_____
_____
_____
_____
_____

Have you been blessed with spiritual DNA siblings
from God?

_____
_____
_____
_____
_____

If so were they closer to you than your natural ones?

_____
_____
_____
_____
_____
_____

God is faithful that promised!!! When all else fail we can rest assured of His consistency and His never ending love.

AJM

So Called Friends

This is a chapter in which I believe everyone who is reading this book can identify. We have all had friends that have come in and out of our lives for one reason or another. That is a part of living and growing. Sometimes we just outgrow people.

However, there are those which remain in which we call true friends. These are the ones we trust to be there to celebrate us, cry with us, laugh with us. These are the friends that you can share your innermost personal stuff with, etc. It is when one of our so called "friends" betrays us that hurt us the most.

This kind of betrayal has happened to me on a couple of occasions. The first betrayal was one in which I had known the person for over twenty-six years. This "friend" knew I was in the midst of a dry season in my life and practically begged me to spend money in which I did not have. They promised they would repay. I was very apprehensive and against my better judgement I did as my friend urged. This decision was perhaps fortified by my "friend" saying she cared about me. I could not help feeling somewhat uncomfortable about the decision. I should have listened to my inner voice. Lack of judgement came back like a vicious little dog and bit me in my butt. My lack of judgement and my "friend's" lack of integrity placed me in precarious situation.

You see I trusted this person as a friend, a person of faith, and a person in ministry. I had never felt so betrayed in my life. In all of this I learned something about myself, which is I am a better friend to most people than they are to me and not everyone operates with integrity. Not only that, people obviously has a different level of meaning and commitment concerning friendships. True friendship requires one to consistently demonstrate integrity, character and loyalty.

In order to keep my heart right after such betrayal I had to forgive this person and ask God to heal my wounds. I began to pray for this person. When you pray for someone that has hurt you or angered you, it's hard to stay upset with them.

It is a process, and sometimes you think you have forgiven only to realize that you really haven't. Only God knows what is truly in our hearts. Sometimes we don't even know. This is why the psalmist David asked God to "search him and know his heart; test him and know his thoughts; and see if there be any wicked way in him and lead him in the way everlasting (Psalm 139:23-24)."

Reflections

Have you ever betrayed a friend?

_____

_____

_____

_____

_____

What did you do to make it right or did you?

_____

_____

_____

_____

_____

Have you ever been betrayed by a friend?

_____

_____

_____

_____

_____

Have you moved beyond the betrayal of a friend? If
so how?

_____

_____

Remember that everything you do and say is a seed that you are sowing in your future! So be mindful!!!
#seedforthought

Preparation for the Test

There is no hurt like church hurt. This is due to the fact that the church is supposed to be the place where you will find acceptance, love and healing. You would never expect it to be the place in which you would get hurt.

As I begin this chapter my mind goes back to my life in Germany. Germany was a place in my spiritual life where I really began to come to know who God really was and develop my relationship with Him. I remember arriving in Germany thinking wow, I'm in another country. While looking out of the window on a sunny spring morning at the lodging bulletin in Pirmasens, Germany, I was in awe of the beautiful green hilly meadows that was unlike anything that I had ever seen before in my life. I began to reflect upon the awesomeness of God. I began to think about His sovereignty and how everything that He does has a purpose. With that in mind I began to think of the possible reasons why He would allow me, a little ghetto girl from Chicago to come all the way to Europe.

As we got settled in to our home in a village called Thelischwiler, I found a job with Service Federal Credit Union on the military post. I thought we were on our way. I had given my life to The Lord while watching the 700 club in ElPaso, Texas a year earlier. I did not have a full understanding of what I did; all I knew was that I wanted a change in my life. A change is exactly what I got!

I developed such a hunger and thirst for righteousness to the point where I would get up at five or six o'clock in the morning and study the word of God for up to three hours a day. Little did I know that all of that fasting and studying was preparing me for the betrayal and adversity that would come my way.

God had blessed me to excel in the things of God very quickly. I was put in leadership positions in the church and served God faithfully. I was committed to doing the things that were assigned to me with a spirit of excellence. God had given me a relationship with the pastor and his wife. There were some people in the church that did not like our relationship and were envious.

I would fast so much that one day my pastor came to me and said "Sister McCafferty, you don't have to fast for everything you want from God." Now how he knew I was fasting I don't know. Only God had to show him unless my breath was giving it away (laughing).

A coworker of mine invited me to a Bible study in which she attended. One day I accepted the invitation and thus began my first relationship with Christian leadership. There I met Elder H. and his family who were the overseers of the Bible study group. They were very nice people and very considerate of the fact that I was married to an unbeliever.

Whenever I would go to Bible study he would call my spouse and thank him for allowing me to attend. Oftentimes he would invite my spouse to go on trips with us or just come over and watch a basketball game with him. The H's soon received orders to leave Germany and I eventually found myself as a member of Church of God in Christ (C.O.G.I.C.).

Reflections

Can you look back at your trials and see that you clearly were being "prepared" for something much bigger?

_____

_____

_____

_____

_____

_____

Write down the things you know the preparation was for:

_____

_____

_____

_____

_____

_____

How do you approach new trials and challenges now?

_____

_____

_____

_____

_____

If you do not change directions you may end up where you're heading.....(unknown)

When Leadership Betrays You

The Lord had blessed me to grow in the word by leaps and bounds. I had a hunger and thirst for the word of God like nothing I had ever known. I would wake up at 5:30am and study the word until it was time for me to get ready for work which was around 9:30am. I began to hear the voice of the Lord talking to me. I began to fast and pray and passionately pursue the Kingdom of God like never before. Little did I know that this was all in preparation for the spiritual warfare that was to follow.

I will call the name of my first real pastor; Pastor Q. Pastor Q was an energetic, zealous and loving man of God. He had a wife that had been wounded in the past and allowed those past hurts to dictate a lot of her behaviors and thought processes. We had pretty much started in this particular ministry around the same time. I served in whatever capacity that I could and was needed in. I was young in The Lord, zealous and on fire for God!! If the word said it I believed it. I could hear a perfect stranger say that they had a headache and I would ask them if they mind if I would pray for them. I would then see the miraculous power of God manifest. This was what my life was like until leadership betrayed me.

One Saturday while in Germany, a minister and his wife were having a barbecue. They called me

to ask if I would pick up another minister in our
congregation that did not have a vehicle. I told them
sure I could do that. Then off we went to a day full of
fellowship, filled with laughter, food and fun. On the
way back the minister asked me if I could pull over so
that he could talk to me. He began to share his heart
about desiring his family to come over to Germany. I
encouraged him in The Lord and shared with him
how The Lord gave me a dream and showed me that
his family would be overseas with him. As I
proceeded to start the car to continue to go home, out
of nowhere the minister tried to grab me and kiss me.
I began to fight him off. He then stopped and
apologized for his behavior. I told him that he needed
some help and that I was going to talk to Elder M
about his actions.

   During the next few weeks the minister that
attacked me went home to get his spouse. I'm not sure
what happened when he got there. The only thing I
knew was that I got a call from the pastor and his wife
stating that they needed to meet with me to talk.
When I met with them they were saying to me: "Ok
Sister McCafferty you can tell us the truth" I was
dumbfounded and asked, "The truth about what?"
They then said that the minister's wife called them
from the states and said he was having an affair with
the missionary in the church. Seeing that I was the
only missionary in the church, one could say it
appeared to be me! I began to tell them the story of

what happened on the way from the barbecue. I
assured them that no such thing had occurred and I
didn't know why she would say that. The pastor and
his wife then told me that they were sitting me down
from ministry because I should have never given him
a ride. They also sat him down from ministry when he
returned which gave the congregation the notion that
we were having an affair.

All this was the enemy's attempt to
assassinate my character. I was devastated!!!! I went
home and cried my heart out. I felt like the pastor and
his wife should have known me better. We had been
in ministry together from the beginning. The couple
that had asked me to give the minister a ride heard of
what happened and came to my home. They saw how
devastated I was and tried to console me. They
hugged me and began to cry with me. They were
apologizing for asking me to give the man a ride. I
had never felt so betrayed in my life.

The talking had started in the church. Haters
and backbiters was chuckling, gossiping and
whispering; wanting to believe so bad that the rumor
was true. I was so wounded that the zeal I once had
for the Lord slowly began to dissipate. To this day
people still believe that rumor. This is because we as
people chose what we want to believe especially
when discernment is lacking.

When I ran into someone I knew from
Germany years later they inquired about the incident.

When I told them what happened they looked at me and said "Jacque the pastor and his wife were the ones that told us that you had an affair with the minister". I could not believe my ears. I felt betrayed all over again. I thought how could they?!!! After all that I did for them and the ministry, why would they?

Reflections

Have you ever been betrayed by church leadership?

_____

_____

_____

_____

_____

_____

If so how did you handle it?

_____

_____

_____

_____

_____

_____

What did you do to allow healing to manifest?

_____

_____

_____

_____

_____

_____

Did the betrayal hinder your relationship to the point of severing ties with your ministry or church? With God?

_____

_____

Do you know where you're going to? Do you like the things that life is showing you?
If not, maybe you should get a new GPS (God's positioning system)!!!!!
#travelingonpoint

The Betrayal Continues

A little more than a year later after the previous incident I left Germany and went to Colorado Springs, Colorado. All I knew was that the Lord Himself was sending me there. Why I did not know, Colorado was clearly not a choice of mine. Unbeknownst to me, the same pastor (Pastor Q) took an early retirement from the military and moved to Colorado Springs to start a ministry. They asked me if I would help with the task. Seeing God had ordered my steps there I just assumed that this was the reason behind it.

As we began to pray and fast for the directions of God concerning the ministry things began to fall in place. The Lord used me to evangelize and bring in people to the church. Things appeared to be going really good. Souls were being won for the kingdom, the ministry was growing and God was blessing.

After returning from a two week vacation with my spouse, I went to church and a couple from another ministry in town that was known for witchcraft was joining our ministry. As I went to give this young lady the right hand of fellowship (a C.O.G.I.C. ordinance), I intended to hug her but the spirit of the Lord took my hug into a handshake. As I walked away I asked God what was that all about? I clearly heard Him say "watch and pray". This had never happened to me before so I made sure that I adhered to the instruction.

A few months later I found out exactly what the Lord was warning me about. This young lady had weaseled her way into a relationship with the pastor and his wife. She convinced them that I did not like her and even lied on me telling them that I said something to her that was clearly not of my character. Whatever the terminology was that she used, it definitely was not words that I would say. This is why it is so important to know those that labor amongst you. This is to help us recognize the enemy who is the accuser of the brethren.

It was a Sunday evening and I had made previous plans to help a woman I worked with move, which was eight months pregnant. She had no one else to help her seeing it was the last minute. This was normally the time in which we would have our evening church service. I called the pastor to let him know that I would not be there. I shared that I promised a co-worker that I would help her move. He expressed to me that that I needed to come to church to meet with him and his wife and that she (the lady that I was helping to move) had people at her job for that. In my head I thought "Wow, now that wasn't a Christian response!!" I proceeded to tell him that I am that help and being a woman of my word I would come to meet with them when I finish helping the young lady with her move.

As I got off the telephone I knew by the Spirit of the Lord that the meeting had to be about some mess. I also knew that due to the spiritual immaturity of the pastor and his wife, they lacked wisdom in how to effectively communicate with people. I also knew of my own spiritual immaturity at that time, in that if someone yelled at me I would yell back. I immediately began to pray that God would keep me and that I would not react to whatever they had to say to me but that I would respond instead.

Once in the meeting the young lady began to state her facts concerning an encounter I had with her after Sunday school. Of course she left out the things that would have made her case invalid. But this is how the enemy works; he likes to bring accusations against the brethren and cause dissention and confusion.

She began to accuse me of something that was not true. I appealed to what she said then it happened; the pastor's wife began to shout at me accusing me of not respecting the pastor because he wasn't Benny Hinn or TD Jakes. All I could think of was, "really??"

At that point it turned personal and had nothing to do with the young lady anymore, so I asked if they could excuse her since this is now about me personally. Once the lady exited the room more yelling and accusations ensued from the pastor's wife. I arose from my seat to leave feeling as if I was no longer going to subject myself to such abuse.

Once I reached the door the pastor yelled at me and said "Sister McCafferty sit down!" I turned and looked at him and responded with disbelief and admonished, "That is how you speak to Rambo (their dog) that is not how you speak to me." At that point I proceeded to walk out of the door then he said in a much more respectful tone, "Sister McCafferty could you please have a seat so that we can finish our conversation?" I turned around to be seated however everything in me was shut off and shut down. All I knew was that this was it for me and this ministry.

Days later I went to their home to let them know that I needed to take a leave of absence from the ministry to allow God to heal my heart. The pastor's wife immediately said that they were trying to build a ministry and that they did not have time for people to be hanging on. She further stated that I needed to be with them in the ministry or just leave altogether. This was just another one of her forms of control.

I proceeded to tell them that in that case I will be leaving their ministry. I went to shake the pastor Q hand to thank him for working with him. He reached out and hugged me telling me that he would always be my pastor and if I ever needed him to let him know. His wife on the other hand gave me what we call a church hug (a hug in which you are barely touch, with perhaps a few lite pats on the back and is most often not sincere) and said that I would be coming back and that I would be driving by their house wanting to come in. Needless to say that never happened thanks to God, I healed and moved pass the betrayal.

I cut ties with some of the people in the church so that it wouldn't be said that I tried to destroy their ministry. This was to no avail seeing that years later it was said that I tried to destroy their church by telling a lot of people to leave. I was devastated to say the least. I was betrayed once again by leadership. I wanted to get away from religious people forever. I even thought about backsliding because I felt that at least in the world you know who your enemies are. They didn't come dressed up using Christian idioms like: "Love you sister", 'God bless you," "I'm blessed and highly favored", etc.

Later I joined another ministry and in my new place of fellowship God began to heal me and make me whole. I was so thankful for being in a fellowship where the Pastor and his wife really walked in the love of God. I learned some valuable lessons about church folk. Most of all I learned how much God truly loved me.

Reflections

Have you ever found yourself betrayed again by the same person?

_____

_____

_____

_____

_____

What do you think caused you to put yourself in the position for this betrayal to be repeated?

_____

_____

_____

_____

_____

What lessons did you learn from this betrayal?

_____

_____

_____

_____

_____

_____

Emerge from your cocoon into the beauty of what God has destined you to be!! Blessings!!!

Overcoming the Betrayal

My relationship with God played a major role in my healing process. I understood the sovereignty of God and what that meant in my life. This intimate relationship with God (my Daddy) changed me by giving me a peace that passes all understanding. Walking in a place of forgiveness and releasing people for the hurt that they caused me was another key element in the process. Choosing to forgive did not mean I had to stay in relationship with the person; it just meant I did not allow that person space in my life to hinder me from moving forward or hinder the plan of God in my life. In other words, I did not need to give the devil a bat to beat me with.

No matter what or who comes or what or who goes I have the peace of God which is my prize commodity. Anything or anybody that disrupts my peace has to go. It is my ruling umpire; it is the most precious thing to me. My relationship with God has giving me a joy that strengthens me in times of weakness and disappointments. I can do as the psalmist David said in Psalms 121:1-2; "look to the hills and know that my help comes from the Lord." Applying the above formula in my life is what helped me to get beyond the betrayal and stand in the midst of adversity.

Reflections

What measures have you taken to get beyond the betrayal in your life?

_____

_____

_____

_____

_____

_____

Are those measures working? If not are you interested in getting additional help?

_____

_____

_____

_____

_____

_____

If the measures are working, what are some of the victories you have experienced?

_____

_____

_____

_____

_____

_____

Conclusion

What's interesting and important is that at this present time my relationship with God is still growing and developing. This is something that I know will never stop until the day that I cease to live. I am constantly evolving into the woman God has destined me to become. I surprise myself by some of the different things I find myself doing and saying.

When I look back over my life I can see the hand of God. Even when I didn't know Him, He knew me. I can see that God was always there intervening on my behalf, looking out for me and protecting me. While standing in the midst of adversity, He was there. The presence of His love helped me to get beyond the betrayal and see the bigger picture. His word says in Hebrews 13:5, "He will never leave you nor forsake you" and I can truly say He is faithful! I continue to stand in adversity but most of all in the blessings of the Lord.

Scriptures for Healing and

Encouragement

Isaiah 41:10 - Fear thou not; for I [am] with thee: be not dismayed; for I [am] thy God: I will strengthen thee; yea, I will help thee; yea, I will uphold thee with the right hand of my righteousness.

Jeremiah 17:14 - Heal me, O LORD, and I shall be healed; save me, and I shall be saved: for thou [art] my praise.

1 Peter 2:24 - Who his own self bare our sins in his own body on the tree, that we, being dead to sins, should live unto righteousness: by whose stripes ye were healed.

Jeremiah 33:6 - Behold, I will bring it health and cure, and I will cure them, and will reveal unto them the abundance of peace and truth.

Isaiah 53:5 - But he [was] wounded for our transgressions, [he was] bruised for our iniquities: the chastisement of our peace [was] upon him; and with his stripes we are healed.

Psalms 103:2-4 - Bless the LORD, O my soul, and forget not all his benefits

Joshua 1:9 - Have not I commanded thee? Be strong and of a good courage; be not afraid, neither be thou dismayed: for the LORD thy God [is] with thee whithersoever thou goest.

2 Timothy 1:7 - For God hath not given us the spirit of fear; but of power, and of love, and of a sound mind.

Psalms 121:1-8 - (A Song of degrees.) I will lift up mine eyes unto the hills, from whence cometh my help.

Psalms 37:4 - Delight thyself also in the LORD; and he shall give thee the desires of thine heart.

Proverbs 30:5 - Every word of God [is] pure: he [is] a shield unto them that put their trust in him.

Psalms 28:7 - The LORD [is] my strength and my shield; my heart trusted in him, and I am helped: therefore my heart greatly rejoiceth; and with my song will I praise him.

Psalms 34:4 - I sought the LORD, and he heard me, and delivered me from all my fears.

1 Thessalonians 5:9-11 - For God hath not appointed us to wrath, but to obtain salvation by our Lord Jesus Christ,

Philippians 4:13 - I can do all things through Christ which strengtheneth me.

About the Author

Addie (Jacque) McCafferty is an ordained minister/prophet of the Gospel. She has been a licensed Evangelist since 1992 and ordained since 2001. She has a call to the Nations and operates in the deliverance and prophetic realm. She teaches others how to hear the voice of the Lord. She is passionate about empowering people to become all that God has birthed them to be in life.

A .Jacque McCafferty is a chaplain at Lexington Medical Center in Columbia in which she received the Harold Von Nessen award for extinguish service. There are no gender and age limitations to her ministry. As a motivational speaker and counselor she utilizes her gifts and talents at conferences, workshops, seminars, schools, crusades, prayer breakfasts, and retreats. She also hosts conferences in which her last conference was called "Shift the Kingdom of Heaven has Come".

She currently is a doctoral candidate of Adult Education and holds a Master of Social Work degree from the University of South Carolina. Also she has Bachelor of Religious Arts in Biblical Studies from Jacksonville Theological Seminary and a Bachelor in Social Work from Limestone College. She is certified with the AACC (American Association of Christian Counselors) and with Restoring the Foundations (RTF) a healing and deliverance ministry as a Focus minister.

A. Jacque McCafferty is a native of Chicago, IL and as a result of her travels around the world she currently resides in Columbia, SC. She currently has no natural children of her own; however she is a spiritual mother of many. Her motto is 'Love like you've never been hurt".

Appendix

More ways to connect with Addie:
You can start by visiting http://addiemccafferty.com,
or email A.McCafferty@aol.com. You can follow on
Twitter @1luvwis and on Instagram
@Jacluv_Wisdom. Through conferences, workshops,
retreats and coaching with Addie you will discover
the tools to equip you to walk in healing and
wholeness to pursue your purpose in life.

Pure Thoughts Publishing, LLC

www.PureThoughtsPublishingLLC.com